A Layman's Guide To Managing Fear

Using Psychology, Christianity, and Non-Resistant Methods

By: Stanley Popovich

A Layman's Guide To Managing Fear
Subtitle: Using Psychology, Christianity,
and Non-Resistant Methods
Copyright © 2003
Stanley   Popovich
All rights reserved.

MountainView Publishing
A Division of
Treble Heart Books
1284 Overlook Dr.
Sierra Vista, AZ 85635-5512

Stanley Popovich's Website
https://www.managingfear.com

ISBN: 1512007803

Table of Contents

Dedication

This book is dedicated to my family, friends, and to God.

INTRODUCTION

Fear is universal. It's not restricted to any age, class, or culture. Everyone deals with fear in varying forms and intensity at one time or another. For some people, fear can easily be managed, and for others, fear can be terrifying and difficult to manage.

Fear is a strong force in people's lives according to Father Howard Campbell. "Fear is an emotion based on experience. Certain events, people, or encounters may activate fear, which, in turn, may lead to anxiety, worry, and panic." A Catholic Priest for more than fourteen years, Father Howard is a pastor in Pennsylvania. He has a Bachelor's Degree in Philosophy and a Master's Degree in Systematic Theology and Divinity.

Typically, fear creates a sense of personal danger. Elderly people may fear loneliness; young people, rejection; and professionals, failure. In many cases, people are afraid of the future such as finding the right career or developing meaningful relationships.

Fear can be a good thing when it protects people from harm. Parents instill fear and define danger when they teach children not to touch fire, run into the street, or play with dangerous animals. "But fear can manifest as anxiety or a phobia" says Father Howard who has considerable experience counseling people facing their fears.

A phobia is a chronic fear based on circumstances that may defy rational or logical thought. A person may be afraid of heights, even though there is no danger of falling. This work doesn't address phobias or any precursors to mental illness. A person with a particular phobia should see a licensed mental health counselor. The author does not intend this work to be a substitute for using the guidance of a mental health professional.

Rather, this book deals with more generalized fears that are common in daily life and presents a general overview of effective methods to combat those fears. The author is not a professional in the psychology or religious fields. However, Stan has over 20 years experience in dealing with fear and anxiety, and he interviewed various mental health counselors in writing this book. Stan then organized all of his research and experiences into one helpful booklet. In addition, Stan's book was reviewed by various mental health professionals before it was published and is designed for helping the every day layman. Many counselors use Stan's book to help their clients.

Fear appears in many different forms depending on the person and the situation. The following sections discuss three powerful but different approaches for managing fear:

☐ General Counseling Techniques
☐ Non-Resistant Methods
☐ Asking For God's Help

The General Counseling Techniques cover a broad range of methods to manage and/or overcome fear. The Non-Resistant Methods are effective when a person's fear is so strong that it's extremely difficult to overcome. Instead of fighting the fear, the person learns to work with it. Asking for God's Help encourages the individual to rely on the power of a personal, spiritual relationship with God. This book then describes how to use all three methods at the same time. The book is then followed by a sampling of professional resources and a few Biblical verses that offer particular messages of comfort and inspiration.

*C*hapter 1

GENERAL COUNSELING METHODS OF DEALING WITH FEAR

Fighting fear is a complex process. The techniques are many and varied. What works for one person may not work for another. The problem? Determining which method will work in each situation, especially when an individual's anxiety is so profound that it's difficult to concentrate on anything but the fear invoking situation. (Of course, it is always wise to consult a mental health professional for advice.)

A collection of proactive steps to overcome a particular fear, the General Counseling Techniques include:

- ☐ Critical Thinking and Deductive Reasoning
- ☐ Build up to the fear in small steps
- ☐ How bad do you want it?
- ☐ Positive Self-Talk
- ☐ Self Imagery
- ☐ How to View a Problem
- ☐ Exercise

Critical Thinking and Deductive Reasoning

For most people, imagination is a wonderful gift. For some, imagination has a dark side, generating terrifying thoughts and anxiety. It can distort thinking, feed fear, and cause worry by making it difficult to determine what is or isn't real. In order to regain control of those feelings, it's important to focus on getting all of the facts of an event, then use critical thinking and deductive reasoning to come up with ways to manage the fear.

The first step is to find out the source of the fear and then determine the root cause. It is best to talk to a professional mental health counselor who can help determine the source of a particular fear.

Next, it's important to get all of the facts of the particular situation. This doesn't get rid of the worry, but can help the individual focus on reality instead of exaggerated assumptions that make no sense. Once the facts are discovered, the individual can focus on the fear that is being experienced and take it apart, piece by piece, using critical thinking and deductive reasoning.

The goals of critical thinking and deductive reasoning are to determine how rational a particular fear is and then come up with solutions and options to manage the fear. Some people tend to fear "what if" situations and worst case scenarios.

Using critical thinking, an individual begins the process by asking themselves what is the worst thing that could happen to them if their fear become a reality. The person then lists all the events that would have to happen in order for the worst case scenario to occur. It's helpful to write those steps without omitting anything. Armed with this list, the person can logically consider how rational it is for all these steps to occur. The individual can then analyze the chances that the situation causing the fear would actually happen.

The final and most important step is to come up with ways to counter apprehension and fear. For every step listed, he or she should analyze the facts and try to find possible solutions that will prevent each step from becoming a reality. The key here is to do a lot of research and take nothing for granted. By coming up with solutions, the individual is, in effect, preventing the worse case scenario from happening. In addition to finding ways to counter the fear, the person is prepared to develop backup plans as a safety net, which helps manage the anxiety causing situation.

This method empowers the person to develop strategies that mitigate the fear. The individual takes charge by having prepared a course of action *just in case* the worst case scenario occurs. The main goal for this entire process is to balance overestimating, negative thoughts with objectivity and reasoning, and to counter the fear with realistic thinking and solutions.

Here's an example of how the process works. John, a college student, is studying to be an engineer. Although John is attending a large and well known engineering school, he's afraid he will get bad grades in his tough classes. John is afraid that he may have to drop out of school and likely end up in a low paying job for the rest of his life. As a result, he's always stressed out. John decides to list of all the events that would have to happen before he'd be forced to leave college and end up in a low paying job—his worse case scenario. Here are the key points John wrote on his list:

1. I might fail a few classes and might not be in good academic standing at the university.
2. I would then get a warning to get better grades.
3. I'd get a few more chances to improve my grades.
4. I'd have to leave school because I couldn't satisfy the minimum academic standards of the university.

5. I wouldn't have the skills or education to get a good job, so I'd have to take a minimum wage job to pay my bills.
6. Without a college education, I'd be stuck at this low paying job for the rest of my life.

Fear of failing in college frightens John, but he's overlooking the facts and the many options available to him. In order to overcome his anxiety, John decides to research the school's policy regarding minimum academic standards and available options. Here's what he learned:

1. Most colleges state that a student must maintain a minimum grade point average in order to be in good academic standing and remain a student at the university.
2. Students get a warning from the university if they're unable to maintain this minimum grade average.
3. John would get a few more opportunities to improve his grades. At this point, John has a variety of options he can use to his advantage.

☐ He could decide that engineering is too difficult and change his major.

☐ Colleges offer students many opportunities to mentor students who are having trouble in their studies. John could take advantage of the study resources his university offers to improve his grades.

☐ He could take fewer classes giving him more time to focus on those courses.

☐ He could transfer to a smaller school where he'd get more individual attention.

4. John's worst case scenario occurs: He's forced to drop out of school because he wasn't able to maintain a good academic

standing. Although John is depressed, he still has some options to avoid ending up in a low paying job.

☐ He might decide to change majors or attend summer school to improve his grades and apply for admission again.

☐ He could apply to a smaller school to get more individual attention.

☐ Instead of pursuing a bachelor's degree, John could go to a community college and study for an associate's degree which would give him a chance to complete basic college classes before focusing on those classes that may be more difficult. Once John gets an associate's degree, he may have a sense of accomplishment and incentive to get a bachelor's degree.

5. John is forced to leave college and get a job. The fact is there are many good paying jobs available that don't require a college degree and there are many successful people who enjoy these jobs. John still has some options.

☐ John could take a skills assessment test to see what kind of career best suits his capabilities and talents. He may like something that doesn't require a college education. Once John evaluates his career options, he should have a better idea of what he wants to do with his life.

☐ He still has the choice of getting additional education. He could choose a technical school or a continuing adult education program.

☐ It's never too late to get a college education. There are a variety of low cost educational programs offered in today's work environment. John also has the option of changing his approach to the situation and giving it another try.

There is one very important fact that everyone should take into consideration: Although a particular fear may be strong and seem real, it's nearly impossible for anyone to predict future events with one hundred percent accuracy. John may be ninety-nine percent correct in predicting what *may* happen as a result of a situation he fears, but all it takes is that one percent to make a world of difference. There are circumstances John can use to his advantage. Unexpected actions or unintended consequences can change the outcome of any situation. This is especially important for people who ask God to help them overcome their problems. Circumstances can change the result of any situation.

Build up to the fear in small steps

At times, just the thought of trying to accomplish a certain goal can invoke fear. The task may seem overwhelming, unbearable, or even impossible. In order to alleviate anxiety, it's a good idea to divide the task into a series of steps. This reduces the fear by breaking it into a series of easily managed pieces. As each of the smaller tasks is accomplished, the individual can analyze when—at what point in the task—the fear began. By facing the fear one step at a time, the fear is better managed. In addition, the person slowly builds themselves up to accomplishing the main task.

Larry Sutton uses this technique to help his clients manage their fears. Sutton, a clinical psychologist with a Ph.D. in counselor education, is also a deacon in the Catholic Diocese. Sutton has counseled many people who were in the process of seeking employment. He first tries to find out the reasons why a particular person is nervous about finding another job. He tries to get all the facts and wants the individual to define the situation he or she is experiencing in as much detail as possible.

Once Sutton gets a better idea of the client's circumstances, he breaks the main objective of finding a job into a series of smaller steps that suits the individual's needs. Sutton then works with his clients to accomplish each of the smaller tasks, one step at a time. As the person becomes successful in completing each of these steps, he or she will get a sense of encouragement that should reduce the fear and worry.

This can be a slow process, however, the person who accomplishes each of the individual tasks is slowly building up his or her confidence to achieve the overall goal. An example of breaking down a job search into a series of smaller tasks likely would include these steps:

☐   Define the kind of job the individual wants.

☐   Create a good resume and cover letter.

☐   Go to the library and research the companies that interest the individual.

☐   Find the manager in charge of hiring at each company.

☐   Send a resume to the manager.

☐   Follow up with a phone call to see if the manager is interested in this person's background.

Eventually, the person can focus on the job interview and, if all goes well, will have a job. Breaking a given task into a series of smaller parts helps to manage the fear. Taking it one step at a time allows a person to concentrate on the task at hand, prevents looking too far ahead, and helps to slowly build up to the main goal.

How bad do you want it?

Sometimes having the determination to accomplish a task can help overcome a particular fear. For example, Joe wants to accomplish a particular task, but anxiety is holding him back. The first thing Joe needs to do is to determine how important is it to achieving his goal.

If Joe isn't interested or motivated to reach his objectives, he may be sidetracked by anxiety and fear. On the other hand, if Joe is determined, it will him to overcome his fear of achieving his goals.

Finding the determination and motivation to do a particular task can sometimes be difficult. Whether it's mowing the lawn on a hot day, shoveling snow during the winter, or going grocery shopping during a thunderstorm, everyone faces tasks they'd rather avoid. When the chore is unpleasant it seems to take forever to get the job done. On the other hand, when an event is fun, it's easy to be enthusiastic and excited. Time seems to pass too quickly.

Accomplishing anything in life can be difficult if a person doesn't have resolve. The important thing to remember is that determination and commitment start from within. At some point in time, everybody must look within to find the incentive to accomplish difficult tasks. Motivation and determination won't erase the fear but will help the person manage it.

Positive Self-Talk

There are times when a person is bombarded with events that appear to happen all at once. Roger, for example, is overwhelmed by competing job demands thrust on him within a few hours. All of a sudden, his mind is churning with anxiety about how to respond to his stressful work situation. These thoughts produce fear and worry that terrify Roger so much that he's not able to complete any of his work. When he gets overwhelmed with fear and anxiety, he tends to get mentally wound up, like a spring that's been twisted to the breaking point.

In order to address his problems, Roger takes a few deep breaths and then coaches himself, using positive statements to remain calm and relaxed. He's learned it's important to slow down and get his mind on something else for a while. He gives himself a mental coffee break by listening to music, taking a walk, or just reading something interesting for a few minutes. This emotional time out distracts Roger from his anxiety and allows him to gain a better perspective on how to manage his problems.

There are many ways a person can achieve positive reinforcement. For example, inspirational phrases and statements are found in many self-help books. "Take it one day at a time" and "I can do it" can be repeated over and over again to the point that a person starts to feel calm and relaxed. Some people pray or repeat some special verses in the Bible that provides peace of mind. This action gives Roger a mental time out from his anxiety, allowing him to get his bearings and reassess how he is going to address his situation. Roger created a notebook that contains several positive phrases that help him relax. Every time Roger finds a meaningful phrase, he adds it to his notebook. Reading these statements will lift his spirits the next time he has a bad day.

Self Imagery

Often, imagination can help overcome fear. When a person has to face an event that produces anxiety and fear, it helps to prepare for it by visualizing the situation. Wayne, a hockey player, is preparing for an upcoming championship final. He's anxious because this game is very important and he's afraid he might not play his best in front of the huge crowd of fans. To reduce his anxiety and fears, Wayne uses his imagination to visualize the game before it actually happens. He goes through the steps, from preparation to playing the game, in his mind. First, Wayne thinks about dressing for the game. He then imagines taking to the ice for some practice shots. During this time, he envisions the anxiety he's facing and how to deal with it. He visualizes his actions and game strategies as he plays the game in his mind, running through different "what if" situations.

This effective way to prepare for the upcoming game is used regularly by many professional athletes. When the actual sporting event takes place, Wayne will have mentally played the game. Visualization is a mental dress rehearsal, allowing him to play through different scenarios and anticipate responses. When it comes time to face his fears, Wayne will be better prepared to accomplish his goals because he's already practiced it in his mind.

A person doesn't have to be an athlete to use this process. Self Imagery can be helpful in managing the fear and anxiety of any upcoming future event.

How to View a Problem

Is the glass half empty or half full? Can a challenging problem become an unexpected opportunity? Is a lifestyle change good news or bad news? There are many ways to view a potentially worrisome problem. It's not easy to be optimistic when facing a problem. Although a person might try to be positive, negative thoughts are difficult to ignore. There are also those people who naturally focus on the negative things that might happen in any potential problem.

For instance, Mary recently lost her job of five years due to budget cutbacks and downsizing. Additionally, the job market is very slow and not many companies are hiring in her area, which will make it even more difficult for her to find a good position.

Mary can view her job search as something bad that happened to her or as an opportunity to better herself and embark on a new career that will be more satisfying. She can look in the want ads for openings, network with friends, go back to school, attend career fairs, or join some networking groups to find a new career.

There are some people who naturally look at situations in a positive manner; over the long term they won't become discouraged. There are also those people who look at their job loss and focus on the negative effects of what may happen. As a problem drags on over time, it becomes more difficult to stay positive and have an optimistic outlook. In these kinds of situations, it helps to broaden the focus of how to look at problems and to change perspective.

Mary, for example, could concentrate on her past accomplishments and future opportunities rather than her current troubles. It's a good time for her to make a list of everything she likes about herself. She should include all of her blessings and everything she is grateful to have in her life. In making this list, Mary shouldn't leave any achievements out or take anything for granted.

Here are some blessings Mary might include on her list:
- ☐ I'm in good health
- ☐ I have a good education
- ☐ I have a family and good friends
- ☐ I'm intelligent
- ☐ I'm capable
- ☐ I'm resourceful

The list can go on and on. Mary might also include all her talents/skills and anything else that makes her feel confident or accomplished. When she finishes writing down all of these positive things, she can look at the list and think about how important these things are to her. The next time she becomes depressed about losing her job, she can take out her list and start to move her focus from the negative problem she's experiencing to the rest of the positive things in her life.

The objective of this exercise is for Mary to focus on her accomplishments and blessings in addition to the one problem she's trying to resolve. In a sense, she is balancing the worry that is created by the negative situation with the positive aspects of her life. By doing this, Mary feels better and has a more optimistic outlook, thereby reducing the worry and fear of her situation.

Exercise

For most people, exercise can reduce worries and clear the mind of negative thoughts. Being active helps Jane channel anxiety and fear into something useful. Most importantly, exercise gives her a fresh perspective in looking at her problems and she's improving her health and enjoying nature. There are many activities like walking, swimming, and biking that help clear the mind. Everyone should be able to find an enjoyable and relaxing activity. *(Note: It is very important to consult with a doctor before doing any kind of exercises so that way you do not hurt yourself.)*

Although some light exercise can help people to feel calm and relaxed, exercise alone can't always get rid of fear and anxiety. Exercise can be very useful, but a person still needs to find a long term solution in dealing with his or her fears and anxieties.

Chapter 2

NON-RESISTANT METHODS OF DEALING WITH FEAR

Although the General Counseling Techniques can be useful for many people, there are times when the effort to get rid of fear makes it that much more difficult to overcome. Specific situations may trigger fear provoking thoughts that are quick to strike and extremely difficult to stop. The Non-Resistant Methods takes a more defensive approach by showing the individual how to reduce the fear's strength by making it easier to manage instead of trying to get rid of the fear.

Instead of getting rid of the thoughts that produce fear, accept the fact that these thoughts will come, but don't dwell or focus on them. The trick is to not analyze those thoughts or figure out why they come. Regardless how scary these thoughts may be, just let them pass. Focusing on fear provoking thoughts may make them more powerful. It helps to think of something else, such as a stop sign, as a reminder to stop focusing on the fearful thoughts. Imagine the shape and color of a stop sign—form a mental picture of the sign—then focus on something positive.

It's helpful to create an imaginary place to put negative thoughts when they appear. Jake uses this technique very effectively. Jake imagines an ice crusted freezer where he can store his negative thoughts. When fearful thoughts creep into his mind, he puts those thoughts into this mental freezer and imagines slamming the door shut. If the disturbing thought returns again, he remembers the freezer and reminds himself that he had this thought before and there is no reason to get upset. There is no need to be startled or scared again. By doing this, Jake minimizes the fear behind those thoughts.

There are times when the number of fearful thoughts coming into a person's mind at the same time is overwhelming. The mind is overrun by "what-if" fears and worst case scenarios. In this case, it's important to remember an individual may be ninety-nine percent correct on predicting what may or may not happen, but that one percent can make the biggest difference. What may seem real is usually not entirely accurate and probably doesn't represent the entire truth.

The difference between a regular thought and an obsessive thought is that an obsessive though is based on fear. Learning how to manage the fear behind an obsessive thought will make it that much easier to get rid of. Talking to a counselor can help with the process.

Chapter 3

ASKING FOR GOD'S HELP TO MANAGE FEAR

God is a powerful ally in the battle to manage fear. It seems obvious to call on the most powerful force in the universe for help, but feeling comfortable enough to ask for God's help often depends upon an individual's relationship with Him. A person doesn't need to be a priest or minister to be close to God. What's important is how the individual views God in his or her own life. It's not difficult to make friends with God:

☐ Read the Bible to gain a better perspective. Gain the wisdom and insight of the importance of God. There are many interesting stories and passages in the Bible; read them to gain a better view of the power of God.

☐ Talk to a trusted priest or minister. By getting the answers to questions about God, a person can become more knowledgeable.

☐ Pray or talk to God. By talking to God on a daily basis, a person can develop a relationship with Him, just like confiding with a close friend.

It's a simple process. Get to know God/Jesus and then develop a foundation of trust in the Lord. Nothing can replace His power and infinite wisdom. He works with us to overcome our problems. God works in mysterious ways and the answers He provides are not always that obvious.

There are many ways a person can ask God to help manage fear. Although a person can try these techniques, working with a priest or experienced minister can help.

Praying at Church

Prayer is the most direct way to communicate with God. Psalm 29:2 encourages prayer:

> *Give to the Lord the glory due His name*
> *Adore the Lord in holy attire.*

A favorite church or chapel, where there are few distractions, is a welcoming place to sit and talk with God. It helped Anna when she was desperate. Nothing seemed to help Anna manage her fears. When she finally decided to ask for God's help, she wasn't sure how to start. She didn't go to church regularly, and she didn't feel comfortable talking to a minister or priest.

One day, Anna walked into a small chapel in her neighborhood. She sat in a pew and gazed around the sanctuary. She saw the open Bible on the altar, the candles, and light filtering through the stained glass windows. After a few moments, she relaxed and sat back in the pew. She happened to see a hymnal on the seat next to her and picked it up. Thumbing through the book, she came upon a hymn whose words seemed to reach out to her.

After sitting there for a few minutes, Anna started praying to God. She talked about her problems as if she were talking to a close friend. She was honest, sharing thoughts and feelings she hadn't been able to tell her family or friends. Finally, she asked for His help and guidance. When she finished praying, she sat in the chapel for a few minutes, absorbing the spiritual surroundings. By spending quality time with the Lord, Anna gained a better perspective of His power and importance in her life.

Prayer can occur anywhere, but it helps to find a place that makes it easier to talk to God without any disruptions. For some people, a church is the best place to go and others feel closer to God by being outdoors in the beauty of nature. The location isn't important. God is everywhere!

Praying outside of church

Christians know God is with them all the time, but sometimes it's difficult to feel the closeness of God outside of church. Many people have a special place to pray or a special prayer that mentally and emotionally prepares them for a conversation with the Lord.

Tom tries to have a quiet time with the Lord every day. To clear his mind and prepare his thoughts for prayer, Tom reads a favorite passage from the Bible. Believers feel God's power in many ways. For example, stories and prayers in the Bible, inspirational books, and hymns can be very helpful.

Inspirational books share God's power through personal stories, messages, prayers, and poems. These all provide excellent ways to get a better perspective of God. Tom reads several books about how God works in other people's lives. Tom is encouraged by their testimonies of God's intervention and how He helps solve problems in the most unexpected ways. These messages of hope helped him understand how God works uniquely in each person's life.

As a constant reminder, Tom put some of his favorite prayers and messages in a personal notebook along with some inspirational statements. The next time Tom feels depressed, he simply opens his notebook and reads the messages and prayers. By feeling close to God and knowing that He is with him, Tom is able to manage his fear. He knows God will help him conquer his problems.

Holding a religious symbol

Sometimes, people need a reminder, something tangible, to help them connect with their spiritual side. For these people, holding or touching something that symbolizes religious or spiritual beliefs provides a tangible link with God.

Joe always keeps a small Bible in his briefcase. When he feels troubled or worried, he's reassured that his Bible is nearby. Joe can reach out and touch the Bible for comfort. Joe feels he has a trusted friend looking out for him. The only difference is his friend is the most powerful force in the universe. Holding onto the Bible or religious symbol acts as a reminder of Joe's beliefs and trust in the Lord. As he faces his particular fears, Joe feels that God is right there with him. He's not facing his demons alone.

Father Howard counsels many people facing life threatening illnesses. His main goal is helping them find the root of their fears. Some of these people have diverse feelings and don't know how to deal with them. They need to first acknowledge their fears to themselves, then talk about their feelings with others. Support and survivor groups, which allow people facing serious illness to share their anxiety or resentment, provide a powerful and therapeutic forum.

Once a person knows the root cause of the fear, Father Howard advocates learning how to manage anxiety and worry. He advises patients facing a life threatening illness to:

☐ Acknowledge the fear and focus on the positive. Don't let negative feelings dominate.

☐ Focus on the good things in life; appreciate the positive minutes and hours of each day instead of taking things for granted.

☐ Take it one day at a time.

☐ Concentrate on God's promises and His Word, and above all, pray regularly.

Father Howard says, "Prayer is not just asking God/Jesus for petitions and getting Him to do things. It is also getting in touch with the Lord and forming a relationship with Him. Prayer can also provide different ways of looking at life and a person who prays, focuses on God."

Father Howard adds, "Prayer may not always change the events around a person, but prayer can change a person's outlook and perception on life." Father Howard reminds everyone that God is omnipotent and all-powerful and He has a great concern for each individual person.

Joe, like most people, finds it easier to put his trust in someone he knows rather than a stranger. The same concept applies with God. Joe realized it was important for his spiritual journey to take the time to include the Lord in his life. It also helped him to talk with his minister. After Joe spent time getting to know God/Jesus, he asked God to use His power to help manage his fears and problems.

These are just a few basic ways to ask for God's help to overcome fear. It's not difficult to build on these techniques and use them to move closer to God.

Chapter 4

USING ALL THREE METHODS AT THE
SAME TIME TO MANAGE FEAR

Combining the General Counseling Techniques, the Non-Resistant Method approach, and the power of God to help overcome fear offers a broad spectrum for managing fear and anxiety. A good starting point includes the following steps:

☐ Understand what is causing the fear. Analyze the situation producing the fear and then ask the question, "What am I afraid of?" Sometimes, the answer to this question will sound rational to the individual but likely will seem irrational to others. It's often difficult to find out the one thing at the root of a particular fear. Talk to a counselor if you need help.

☐ Develop a game plan to find the answers that will help manage the fear.

☐ Gather all available information and resources about the problem.

☐ Find out what information is useful in solving the problem.

☐ Apply the information to solve the problem. Each approach tackles fear in its own way. By using a combination of the three methods, a person becomes more versatile and efficient in dealing with fear.

Here's how the process works for Mike. Although Mike is a very outgoing and successful businessman, he's afraid of speaking in front of large groups of people. His anxiety is jeopardizing his opportunity for a major promotion. He asked God to help him overcome his problem, read some self-help books, and eventually talked to a psychologist. The psychologist recommended he slowly build up to his goal by speaking in front of a small number of people and gradually building up to larger audiences. Over time, Mike became comfortable speaking to larger and larger groups of people. Eventually, Mike became confident enough to speak to large audiences.

A few months later, Mike saw his doctor for a yearly check up. The doctor told him that he needs to start taking better care of his health or else, as he gets older, he will develop serious health problems. After talking to the doctor, Mike worried constantly about his health and potential future medical problems. Even though he followed his doctor's advice, Mike couldn't stop worrying about his future health.

He was so consumed by his fears that other aspects of his life began to suffer. He talked to a psychologist, but it didn't seem to give him the peace of mind he needed. He bought some self-help books and read them carefully. Realizing he needed something more, Mike asked God for help. Because he wanted to develop a closer relationship with God, Mike prayed more frequently, went to church regularly, and read the Bible. Mike is reassured when he realizes God is always with him and will always be there for him throughout the rest of his life.

When fear changes, it's often helpful for the person to change the approach used to deal with it. Mike had two reasons for anxiety. First, he was afraid of speaking in front of a large group of people. Secondly, he worried his health would deteriorate as he aged. He was able to control his fear of speaking in front of people by using a basic psychology technique. When anxiety about his health consumed him, he had a difficult time finding an effective way to overcome it. Instead, he shifted approaches and decided to ask for God's help to overcome his fears. During this whole process, he addressed God about both his fears, asking the Lord to lead him in the right direction. There comes a point in time when everything a person can do to solve a problem has been done and the best choice is to leave it in the hands of God.

"The end result is that God is in control and he will take care of us" says Rev. Larry Isbell, pastor of a church in Pennsylvania. Isbell, with a Master's Degree in Divinity, has been a pastor for sixteen years. When he talks to people about their fears, Isbell tries to determine the nature of their fear and uncover why they are afraid. He tries to get a good idea of the person's life and the specific situation creating the fear. He then works with the person to overcome their fear. Sometimes, he'll recommend a psychologist, therapist, or counselor.

Isbell stresses that in the end, life is not secure and only in God is there true security. There is the faith perspective and belief that no matter what happens, God has us in His hands.

When fear and anxiety become really tough, the techniques and concepts described in this book should help, but the best solution is asking for God's help. This means trusting in God. It can be difficult to have faith in God when things are going wrong. The power of prayer can't be overestimated. Prayer is very effective to help overcome fear and other mental health issues.

No one can hide from God. If God wants something to happen, it will happen regardless. Although some people think they can avoid danger by playing it safe, only God decides what does and doesn't happen. Alice, for instance, is afraid to drive her car on any major highways or through intersections near her home because she is afraid there's more of a chance she could be injured in a car accident. She decides to drive only on local roads where there isn't a lot of traffic. This works for her and she feels safe.

Although Alice is trying to reduce her chances of getting into an accident by not driving in traffic, she doesn't realize that if God wanted something to happen, it would happen. It doesn't matter whether Alice drives her car on a local road with no cars or she drives her car on a major highway during rush hour. There is nothing Alice could do if God wanted certain events to occur. Alice can even stay at home where it's safe, but that wouldn't prevent something from happening.

Alice is wise to do what she can to avoid dangerous things, however there comes a time when events are in God's hands.

"Trusting in God is like knowing and trusting a person" says Joel Reed, a Biblical Scholar who has a Master's Degree in Arts and Religion. Throughout the Bible, there are stories about how people should trust in God. According to Reed, everyone who trusts in God believes that He is all-powerful. "That means God loves and cares about each person, knows what is best in each life, and will always be with His flock."

"Trusting in God is a process, not a one time event. Trust in God builds, first by trusting Him with the little things in life and by knowing Him. Over time, the trust grows and becomes easier" Reed advises. Trusting in God can be difficult when events don't work out, however it's important to be honest with God and tell Him that it's hard to trust. It helps if the person reaffirms his trust and belief that God will help him.

Reed believes the person needs to have faith which is the belief and acceptance in the promises of God, and the belief in God's ability to fulfill those promises. "When it really comes down to it, a person needs to believe in the promises of God and also be convinced God will be there for him. If an individual doesn't believe that God will help him, it will make it that much harder to trust that God will solve his problems" Reed says.

When the shadows of doubt and darkness begin to fall on us, we need to remind ourselves to trust in God by telling ourselves this phrase, "I will rely on the Lord." Whenever adversity and trouble come, a person should not rely on his or her own intelligence, but instead, rely on the Lord. The Bible says to trust in God and if the person believes in God and His promises in the Bible, then that is the advice he or she needs to follow.

Chapter 5

GETTING THE HELP NEEDED
TO MANAGE FEAR

It's one thing to read about managing fear; it's much harder to apply these methods in real life. The first step, and sometimes the most difficult, is admitting there's a problem. Whether it's fear and worry or alcohol and drugs, the individual must realize there's a problem that requires help. Finding excuses or people to blame will not make any problem go away. Help is available. It's up to each person to take advantage of it. In today's society, there's a wide range of expertise and assistance and all it takes is a little bit of effort on the person's part to find it.

When the decision is made to seek help, the individual needs to find the people or organizations with the experience to solve his or her particular problems. There are many ways to find mental health professionals. Physicians, hospitals, and local support groups can provide recommendations. Similarly, a person who needs the services of the clergy can look in the phone book for churches in the area or ask friends and neighbors about pastors they may know.

Once the individual finds the person and/or organization with the resources and credentials needed to address the problem, the next step is to follow through. This requires action and the willingness to take advantage of help that is available and patience, persistence, and the desire to solve the problem on the individual's part. It's never easy in fixing your mental health issues, however you can be successful by taking it one step at a time.

The following is a small list of organizations and Stan's website that provide important information on dealing with fear, anxiety, depression, stress, addiction and other mental health issues:

The World Federation for Mental Health
P.O. Box 16810
Alexandria, Virginia, 22302-0810
https://wfmh.global/
This is an international non-government organization that promotes mental health and tries to prevent mental illness in the world population.

National Institute of Mental Health
6001 Executive Boulevard, Rm. 8184, MSC
9663 Bethesda, MD 20892-9663 USA
http://www.nimh.nih.gov
The mission for the National Institute of Mental Health is to find treatments that prevent mental illness through the use of research. This website has a great deal of information on many mental health topics.

Freedom From Fear
308 Seaview Ave.
Staten Island, New York 10305 USA
http://www.freedomfromfear.org
Freedom From Fear is a national, not-for-profit mental health association that helps people with anxiety and depressive illnesses.

National Health Information Center
U.S. Department of Health and Human
Services P.O. Box 1133
Washington, DC 20013-1133
http://www.health.gov/nhic
This is a health information referral service that places people that have questions about mental health with those organizations that can provide them with the answers.

National Mental Health Association
2001 N. Beauregard Street, 12th
Floor Alexandria, VA 22311
http://www.nmha.org
A not-for-profit organization that tries to improve the mental health of Americans through education, research, and service. Also has referrals for organizations that provide local treatment.

The Center for Mental Health Services
Substance Abuse and Mental Health Services
Administration Room 12-105
5600 Fishers Lane
Rockville, MD 20857
https://www.samhsa.gov

Leads the national systems that deliver mental health services and provides treatment and support services for adults and children with mental illness.

The Website of Author, Stanley Popovich

Stan provides a lot of helpful advice on managing your anxieties and fears under the article and blog section of his website. A must read!!

https://www.managingfear.com

A neighborhood library or bookstore can provide additional information on problems. Reading is an important way to get informed and often provides helpful insight into problems. It's also helpful, when working with a mental health professional, to keep notes on the advice a counselor gives to you.

SUMMARY

Following is a brief summary of key points in this book, followed by a list of Biblical scripture that deals with fear and trusting in God.

Fear skews perception. While the consequences of a particular anxiety or fear may seem incredibly real, there are usually other factors and circumstances that can't be anticipated and can affect the result of any situation.

Nothing is 100 percent certain. A person may be ninety-nine percent correct in predicting what may happen as a result of fear, but all it takes is that one percent to make a world of difference. What may seem real usually isn't entirely accurate in terms of the facts of a given situation and, generally, it's not the entire truth.

Fact or fiction? When encountering a particular fear, it's very important to get all the facts. In any situation, never assume something is true until all the facts are available. The fact gathering process can help a person focus on the reality of a situation instead of focusing on exaggerated assumptions. In order to overcome fear and negative thoughts, write down the thoughts or event that is producing the anxiety. The next step is to write down all the ways that will help to counter the fear and make the thoughts or events less fearful. Be realistic and ask questions that will maintain objectivity and realistic thinking.

Take it one day at a time. Concentrate on the present rather than worrying about tomorrow and the day after. When overwhelmed by fear and anxiety, slow down and take a few deep breathes and then try to think about something else. Some people use positive statements to calm themselves. It helps to do something enjoyable, such as reading, playing a game, or listening to music. This distraction provides a fresh perspective on the situation.

The glass IS half full. A person has the choice to view problems in a negative or in a positive way. There will always be problems in life, so try to focus on the positive things and blessings in life. Being happy is a choice. Choose to be happy. Don't take anything for granted.

Don't worry about a problem. Think the problem through to find the answers. Attack fear logically. What did worrying ever accomplish? Nothing! Worry doesn't solve problems. Worry just creates them.

Practice makes perfect. In order to develop self-confidence, practice doing the task at hand.

Marginalize fear. Regardless of how scary negative thoughts may be, don't focus or dwell on them. Focusing on frightening thoughts makes the fear stronger and more powerful. It helps to come up with an image, a red light or stop sign, that serves as a reminder to stop dwelling on fearful thoughts.

Ask God to help. Pray and God will work in His own way. It's good to think back and remember the other times He has helped. Have faith in the unlimited and unimaginable power of the Lord. Focus on God instead of worrying. The omnipotent and all-powerful God has a great concern for each individual person, and He is in control. A person can build trust in God by knowing and trusting Him with the little things in life. Over time, the trust will grow and it will become easier to trust in God.

Learn from experience. Dealing with fear can be a learning experience if the individual makes the effort to understand what it is about a given situation that triggers the anxiety and which coping skills are most effective to manage the fear. If the effort to control and manage the fear doesn't work out the first time, don't give up. Managing fear, like so many things in life, takes practice. It's helpful to review the techniques offered in this guide, focus on ways to improve coping skills, and think positively.

Think outside the box. Sometimes solving a particular problem requires a different approach, a new way of doing things. The more versatile a person is, the better able he or she can solve problems. If one approach doesn't work, try another. Be open to new ways of thinking and attacking problems. Never quit. Always be persistent.

Help is everywhere. All kinds of help are available in today's society, however it's up to the individual to take advantage of it. A person must be willing to seek help and then use it.

Biblical scriptures that offer comfort

Following are some Biblical scriptures that deal with fear and trust in God. A person who uses the Bible might find this very helpful. The purpose of this section is to review what the Bible says about fear.

Be strong and courageous! Do not be afraid of them! The LORD your God will go ahead of you. He will neither fail you nor forsake you.
Deuteronomy 31: 6

I command you—be strong and courageous! Do not be afraid or discouraged. For the LORD your God is with you wherever you go."
Joshua 1: 9

Even when I walk through the dark valley of death, I will not be afraid, for you are close beside me. Your rod and your staff protect and comfort me.
Psalm 23: 4

Can all your worries add a single moment to your life? Of course not! And if worry can't do little things like that, what's the use of worrying over bigger things? "Look at the lilies and how they grow. They don't work or make their clothing, yet Solomon in all his glory was not dressed as beautifully as they are. And if God cares so wonderfully for flowers that are here today and gone tomorrow, won't he more surely care for you? You have so little faith! And don't worry about food—what to eat and drink. Don't worry whether God will provide it for you. These things dominate the thoughts of most people, but your Father already knows your needs. He will give you all you need from day to day if you make the Kingdom of God your primary concern. "So don't be afraid, little flock. For it gives your Father great happiness to give you the Kingdom.
Luke 12: 25-32

Commit everything you do to the LORD. Trust him, and he will help you.

Psalm 37: 5

The LORD is righteous in everything he does; he is filled with kindness. The LORD is close to all who call on him, yes, to all who call on him sincerely. He fulfills the desires of those who fear him; he hears their cries for help and rescues them
Psalm 145: 17-19

Don't be afraid, for I am with you. Do not be dismayed, for I am your God. I will strengthen you. I will help you. I will uphold you with my victorious right hand.
Isaiah 41: 10

Then Jesus got into the boat and started across the lake with his disciples. Suddenly, a terrible storm came up, with waves breaking into the boat. But Jesus was sleeping. The disciples went to him and woke him up, shouting, "Lord, save us! We're going to drown!" And Jesus answered, "Why are you afraid? You have so little faith!" Then he stood up and rebuked the wind and waves, and suddenly all was calm. The disciples just sat there in awe. "Who is this?" they asked themselves. "Even the wind and waves obey him!"
Matthew 8: 23-27

Jesus came and told his disciples, "I have been given complete authority in heaven and on earth. Therefore, go and make disciples of all the nations, baptizing them in the name of the Father and the Son and the Holy Spirit.
Matthew 28: 18-20

What do you mean, 'If I can'?" Jesus asked. "Anything is possible if a person believes."

Mark 9: 23

"I am leaving you with a gift—peace of mind and heart. And the peace I give isn't like the peace the world gives. So don't be troubled or afraid."
John 14: 27

And we know that God causes everything to work together for the good of those who love God and are called according to his purpose for them.
Romans 8: 28

Don't worry about anything; instead, pray about everything. Tell God what you need, and thank him for all he has done. If you do this, you will experience God's peace, which is far more wonderful than the human mind can understand. His peace will guard your hearts and minds as you live in Christ Jesus.
Philippians 4: 6-7

Personal Notes

This book contains valuable information in managing fear and anxiety. At this point, the reader should use the concepts herein to help develop a personal strategy and find the ways to solve his or her own problems. Write down any useful or more personal information to help you develop these strategies. It's a start.

_____

_____

_____

_____

_____

_____

_____

_____

_____

_____

_____

_____

_____

_____

About the Author

Stan Popovich is a graduate of the Pennsylvania State University and has a background in the computer and business fields. Mr. Popovich noticed that many people struggle with fear and anxiety and that getting quality and complete information on these issues was sometimes difficult. As a result, Mr. Popovich used his analysis, research, and writing skills from his education at the Pennsylvania State University to find the many different ways to help manage fear and anxiety.

Mr. Popovich is not a professional in both the psychology or religious fields, however he has worked tirelessly to find ways to manage fear through extensive research and interviewing various mental health professionals in both of those fields. Mr. Popovich has over twenty years personal experience in using a combination of these managing fear techniques. He organized his information into a helpful booklet, a tool to be used in daily management of fears by young and old. Stan's book was reviewed by various mental health counselors before it was published.

Visit Stan's website at https://www.managingfear.com for more helpful advice.

Made in the USA
Middletown, DE
25 March 2019